DRILLS AND SKILLS FOR YOUTH BASKETBALL

Rich Grawer
Sally Tippett Rains

COACHES
≡CHOICE

ISBN: 1-57167-190-0
Library of Congress Catalog Card Number: 96-69298

Cover Design and Diagrams: Deborah M. Bellaire
Developmental Editor: Joanna Wright
Director of Production: Michelle A. Summers
Photos: Interior—Drew McDaniel

Coaches Choice Books is a division of: Sagamore Publishing, Inc.
                                             P.O. Box 647
                                             Champaign, IL 61824-0647
                                             (800) 327-5557
                                             (217) 359-5940
                                             Fax: (217) 359-5975
                                             Web Site: http//www.sagamorepub.com

DEDICATION

*For my dad, Tony, who through great personal
sacrifice, gave me the opportunities in my
grade school and high school years to develop
my love and appreciation for sports and the
values they impart.*

ACKNOWLEDGMENTS

Thanks to the following people without whose efforts this book would not have been possible:

Brian Grawer, Manoli Potsou, and Michael Musick for helping demonstrate the fundamentals of the game in the book's photos.

Drew McDaniel, a Clayton High School Student, for his professional skill in photographing the action shots in the book.

All the fine players whom I have had the privilege of coaching at the high school and collegiate levels.

All the young men and women who have attended my basketball camps and clinics over the last thirty years, providing me with wonderful teaching opportunities and examples of the effectiveness of my teaching methods.

My many assistant coaches, without whose help I never would have been able to enjoy and succeed in my profession.

My wife, Theresa, for her role in keeping the family together when I was out pursuing my love of coaching.

My six children; Rick, Shelly, Kevin, Laura, Tim, and Brian, for being the pride and joy of my life and the *best* student-athletes I have ever been associated with.

CONTENTS

The purpose of this book is to help kids, parents, and coaches learn the game of basketball. Too often, players go out to practice on their own and do not know what to do or how to do it. They simply go to their backyard and shoot the basketball—and, at that, shoot it incorrectly or without actually accomplishing much. Parents often want to help their kids to become better basketball players, but they do not know what to teach, how to teach it, and how to make sure that the youngster is practicing the skill the correct way. Many coaches simply take the job because no one else will do it. They have to rush to the library and try to find several books to help them teach the basic skills of the game.

This book will help in all of these situations.

No matter if the youngster is eight or eighteen, there are drills, activities, and pictures in the book to explain all the skills necessary to take a kid and help him or her become an actual basketball player. Even a youngster can pick up the book and see how the correct skills of the game are to be practiced.

Coaches can use the book not only to teach skills but also to learn how to set up and run a practice session—with or without a gym—to address parents' concerns, and to make the game fun for kids. No matter if you are a coach of a youth league team, junior high, or high school team, there is something for you in *Drills and Skills for Youth Basketball*.

—RG

CHAPTER 1

The Coach's Responsibility

There are as many different types of basketball coaches as there are levels of basketball. Coaches range from highly paid professionals to volunteers, from veteran former players to novices who have never taken a jumpshot. Each coach has taken on a formidable task. This responsibility is perhaps most intimidating at the youth level, where coaches are often expected to teach their players the fundamentals of basketball and can have a significant impact on the children's lives. This job is especially difficult for those parents who accepted a coaching position so their children would have the opportunity to play, but know little or nothing about the game of basketball, and even less about coaching it.

There are several questions coaches should consider before their first practice. What skills are important for their players to learn, and what is the best way to teach them? How can they maximize their practice time? How do they set up a practice schedule? What if there are times when no gym is available for practice? Should they play to win or let the kids play for fun? These are important considerations for the youth basketball coach that will be addressed in this book.

The youth coach's job primarily involves teaching. Teaching does not take place on its own; it is an art. The four basic steps of the learning process are explanation, demonstration, imitation, and repetition.

Explanation
The first step in teaching is explanation. Coaches should explain to their players what they want them to learn and use terminology the children can understand. It is also important for coaches to remember that children have short attention spans and tailor their explanations accordingly.

Demonstration
The second step in teaching is demonstration. After explaining the skill they want to teach, coaches should demonstrate it for their players. There are several ways to accomplish this step. If coaches are comfortable performing the skill, they can demonstrate it themselves. If not, they can ask someone else to come to practice or use one of their players to demonstrate the skill, or use a videotape.

Imitation

After demonstrating the skill, coaches should give players the opportunity to practice it themselves. During this step, it is important that the players practice performing the skill correctly. Coaches should observe the players carefully and make corrections when necessary.

Repetition

The final step in the learning process is repetition. The players should practice the skill regularly to become familiar with it. Drills and games can be used to keep that practice from becoming monotonous.

Coaches who have never played basketball must be creative when it comes to teaching their players certain skills and techniques. They can show portions of instructional videos to the children and point out the correct techniques. They can also ask a friend or another parent for assistance. If they have players who are skilled in certain techniques, they can use those players to demonstrate for the rest of the team.

It is also difficult for these coaches to observe each player's techniques during practice, especially if they are the only coach for 10 or 12 players. Because bad habits are hard to break, it is important that children learn good habits early. One way for coaches to observe all their players is to videotape a practice or a game. They can then watch the tape either alone or with their players, looking for proper technique. If they watch the tape with their players, coaches should be extremely careful in their praise and criticism of individual players.

Coaches should remember that kids will not catch on to a new skill right away, nor will they all learn at the same rate. It will take several practices before most of them are familiar with a skill, and some kids may never really become comfortable with it. Basketball is a difficult game for kids to play. It can also be intimidating. The proximity of the fans and the low number of players on the court at a time tend to expose players who have difficulty with such fundamentals as dribbling, passing and catching, or shooting, and can make these players feel inadequate or embarrassed. Helping players to have fun and building their self-esteem is another important responsibility of youth coaches.

CHAPTER 2

Getting to Know the Court

Simple diagrams can be very helpful in explaining plays to kids. To avoid confusion, coaches should be consistent whenever they use basketball terminology or diagram symbols. Diagram 2-1 illustrates common terms for different areas of the basketball court.

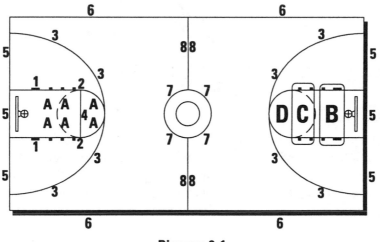

Diagram 2-1

The following symbols are standard when diagramming basketball plays.

1—Block
2—Elbow
3—3-point line
4—Foul line
5—End line/base line
6—Side line

7—Center jump circle
8—Mid court/ ½ line/ 10-second line
A— 3-second area/multipurpose area/paint/key
B—Low post
C—Mid post
D—High post

Offensive player— **o**

Defensive player— **X**

Ball/cone—　　　　　　**●**　△

Movement of a player without the ball—　——

Movement of a player dribbling the ball—　⌇⌇

Movement of a player to set a screen—　——|

Movement of the ball via a pass—　- - -

The Multipurpose Area

Many games are won or lost in the multipurpose area of the court; that is, the free throw lane up to the top of the key (Diagram 2-2). The team that gets the ball into this area the most and controls this area offensively and defensively will usually win the game.

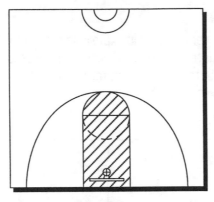

Diagram 2-2

Coaches should realize the importance of getting the ball inside. Getting to the lane in basketball is like establishing the running game to set up the pass in football. If a basketball team does not get the ball in the multipurpose area and establish an offensive threat there, the outside players will never be open for an uncontested 12-15-foot jumpshot.

In addition to high-percentage shots, the multipurpose area also presents good passing opportunities. From the high-post area, near the free throw line, passes can be made to players cutting inside or stepping into the gaps created by sagging defenses (Diagram 2-3).

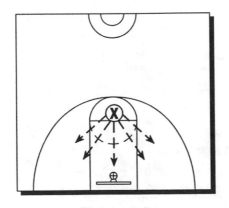

Diagram 2-3

A player in the multipurpose area may also dribble penetrate to the hole. This penetration opens passing and cutting lanes and creates opportunities to draw fouls on the defense. Shots taken in the multipurpose area generally create more favorable offensive rebounding opportunities than shots taken from other areas. Using the multipurpose area of the court is the key to making things happen.

CHAPTER 3

Running a Successful Practice

At the first practice of the season, it is important for the coach to go over basic team rules and guidelines with the players. When working with younger children, it is a good idea to include the parents in this meeting. The coach should let everyone know what is expected of them up front, rather than determining the rules as the season progresses.

Because coaches have a limited amount of practice time, it is important that they be able to get their players' attention quickly. There are several ways of doing this.

1. Whistle
Players stop whatever they are doing and get into a basketball stance near the coach whenever they hear three short blasts of the whistle. The players stand with their feet shoulder-width apart, backs nearly straight, knees and shoulders facing forward, and hands in front of the chest with the palms out. The head should be erect and slightly forward over the feet. The players are expected to listen to all instructions given and then move quickly to follow directions.

Besides getting the players' attention, this technique helps the children develop a proper stance even without the basketball and trains the muscles to memorize the correct stance. Players use this stance to guard, protect the ball, dribble, pass, catch, shoot, and jump.

2. Last Person
In this technique, whenever coaches want the players to gather and listen, they call, "last person." The players are expected to stop whatever they are doing and hustle over to stand or take a knee near the coach. The last person to arrive is penalized in a manner determined by the coach.

3. No Talk Rule
Telling the team there will be no talking for the first five minutes of practice establishes an environment that makes it easier for the coach to get the players' attention. Players who break the rule will be penalized in a manner determined by the coach.

4. Hard Conditioning Drill

Beginning practice with a drill that increases the players' heart rate and breathing is another good attention-getter. While the players are catching their breath, they are less likely to be talking among themselves. This recovery period is a good time for the coach to give directions.

5. Soft Talk Technique

Many coaches get their players' attention by speaking in a low voice that can only be heard if everyone is quiet. Coaches who use this technique should make sure the players really have to concentrate to hear them.

Points to Remember When Coaching Young Players

- Because of their limited practice time, coaches should develop and use drills that combine various skills and are fun, easy to understand, and relatively short (ten minutes maximum).

- Coaches should be observant and correct players when they are performing techniques incorrectly.

- Coaches should have a written practice plan when they come to practice. They should get their players' attention and keep the players on task to stay on schedule.

- Coaches should teach players the triple-threat position, from which they can dribble, pass, or shoot. Players should face the basket and protect the ball. The coach should teach the kids to catch the ball with their knees bent, pivot, tuck the ball, face the basket, and rock and fake.

- Players should learn to run hard, especially when making the transition from offense to defense. It may be best to have all players sprint to the lane and then fan out into their normal defensive positions.

- For younger players, the basic goal on defense should be to protect the basket. The opponent should be forced to win with outside shots. The coach should emphasize not allowing lay-ups and not committing fouls.

Teaching Players to Pivot

Pivoting is an essential part of the game of basketball. It is important for young players to understand that when they are holding the basketball, they are allowed to move one foot while keeping the other foot stationary. The stationary foot is called the pivot foot.

Photo 3-1

The critical component of pivoting is balance. Players should stay in the triple-threat position facing the basket and protect the ball. While pivoting, they should be careful not to lean too far forward or back, or they will lose their balance. The player's head should be centered over the body. Players should also learn to fake with the head, shoulders, feet, and ball. Fakes should be short, quick, and realistic, not exaggerated. When faking, the player should remain in the triple-threat position.

Pivoting Drill

Players should line up on one baseline, sprint to the half-court line, and come to a jump stop in basketball position. They should hold this position until the coach gives a command, such as "right foot, rear pivot" or "left foot, front pivot." The designated foot becomes the pivot foot, and the designated direction is the direction in which they pivot. Coaches should make sure the players do not raise their heads and shoulders when executing the pivot. It should be a smooth 180-degree turn with very little upper body movement. After executing the pivot, players should be in a balanced triple-threat position opposite the direction from which they started.

How to Run a Practice

The secret to running a successful practice is to maximize action time and minimize talking time. Transitions should take place quickly, and the maximum length of drills should be 10 minutes. Young players have short attention spans, so coaches should make the most of the time when they are interested.

At the beginning of the season, coaches should set yearly goals. During the season, they should set daily goals. Every practice should have an area of emphasis. Coaches should teach skills by breaking them down into parts, then putting them back together. Each practice should end with a fun or competitive activity.

Sample Practice Plan

Date:
Daily Practice Emphases:
1.
2.

Practice Number:
Time Started:
Time Ended:
Total Time:

Time	Practice Activity	Coaching Emphases

A Practice Without a Gym

Too often coaches at every level complain about the lack of gym time to practice. I myself had this problem when I was coaching at the high school level. Even though my program at DeSmet High in St. Louis was the best in the state—we had won three large school state championships and 63 games in a row—there were times when my gym was unavailable due to parents' meetings, school dances, auctions, etc. Undeterred, I would go to the cafeteria or a stage in the auditorium and move tables and chairs around until I had created enough space to have a one-hour workout.

10 mins: Stretching and loosening up

5 mins: Jumping drills with jump ropes or small hurdles

10 mins: Every player has a ball—work on stationary dribbling/ballhandling skills

5 mins: 2-man passing drills

5 mins: Tipping the ball against the wall; use one hand held straight up, locked at the elbow; tip ball against the wall with a flick of the wrist. See how many consecutive tips while jumping can be made without losing the ball.

5 mins: Triple-threat position—work on the head and shoulder fakes, pass/fakes, and shot fakes

5 mins: Defensive stance and defensive slide drills

5 mins: Have a defender guard the player with the basketball. The offensive players have to pivot and rock, protecting the ball by swinging their arms. The defenders work on staying down in the basketball position and try to distract the offensive players by placing their hand where the basketball is.

10 mins: Form shooting—lie on your back and shoot the ball upward. Players pair off with a partner and while sitting on chairs, shoot the ball back and forth. The emphasis should be on the correct technique and form of the elbow, wrist (cocked), the follow through and the rotation of the basketball.

5 mins: Conditioning—run the stairs, run outside or run the hallways

This concludes a crisp, sixty-five minute workout which emphasizes the skills of the game—a workout for which you do not need a gym or a basket. I have always felt that where "there's a will, there's a way." I never like to hear coaches complain that they do not have a practice facility. I have even done this same workout with 15 players in my basement.

CHAPTER 4

Developing Players

Photo 4-1

The primary task of a youth basketball coach is to develop a child who wants to play basketball into a basketball player. To be a player, a youngster must have the following characteristics:

- Agility and coordination: The youngster should be able to run, jump, stop, stay under control, catch while running, remain balanced, and move quickly.
- Ability to play in basketball position: Youngsters should be able to get in triple-threat position, pivot, and slide.
- Ability to dribble the basketball
- Ability to catch and pass the basketball
- Ability to shoot, especially lay-ups and short shots, using the backboard
- The player should understand the game and be coachable.

At the youth basketball level, winning is not what coaching is all about. The development of players' skills should be the measure of a coach's success. If at the end of the season a youngster who could not dribble the ball has learned to dribble with some efficiency, or a child who was awkward and clumsy has learned to play in a balanced triple-threat position, then the coach and player have been successful.

Basketball Coaching Absolutes According to Rich Grawer

- Basketball success is predicated on execution of fundamentals.
- The coach is the teacher. The subject is fundamentals.
- The well-conditioned team can always stay competitive.
- At lower levels winning is more related to good offense.
- Simple is better.
- Players draw confidence from their coach. The coach should always try to appear organized, alert, knowledgeable, and poised.
- Breakdown drills are essential to team success.
- Players need motivation to work on their own but at the coach's pace.

Agility, Coordination and Quickness Exercises

Agility, coordination, and quickness are important traits in basketball players. Coaches should understand the definitions of these qualities. Agility is the ability to move with coordinated quickness and smoothness. Coordination is the ability to move different parts of the body in harmony. Quickness is not pure speed, as many people suppose, but rather the ability to make rapid movements.

The following drills and exercises can be used to develop agility, coordination and quickness in the athlete. They should be performed several times a week to be effective. Coaches should pick and choose the ones they feel will be most beneficial to their players.

Small Hurdle or Cone Drills

The coach should place 5-12 hurdles or cones 2-3 feet apart. Hurdles actually work best for these drills because it is easier for players to cheat with cones. To make small hurdles to use in the drills, a coach can take two cones and attach a wood strip across the top. Another option for coaches is to make small hurdles out of plywood. Using two pieces of wood, the coach can attach one piece of wood to a base to form an upside-down T, or cut a groove into the base to insert the upright board into. The hurdles should be between 8 and 12 inches high depending on the age of the players. The coach can have the players run several drills using the hurdles or cones.

- Players weave in and out of the hurdles in figure-eight fashion as quickly as they can.
- Players jump off both feet over the hurdles. This drill helps them learn to maintain their balance.
- Players pick up their right leg and jump over the hurdles with their left leg. This drill helps them learn to maintain their balance. After a designated number of repetitions, the players pick up their left leg and jump over the hurdles with their right leg.

- Players run the hurdle course and jump over the hurdles without stopping (Photo 4-2).
- Players alternate jumping off the right foot and jumping off both feet. After a specified number of repetitions, players alternate jumping off the left foot and jumping off both feet.
- Players repeat all of the above while holding a basketball at chest level.
- Players repeat one through five above while holding a basketball above their head with their arms straight up and elbows locked (Photo 4-3).
- Players repeat one through five above with a two- to three-pound barbell weight in each hand.
- Players jump over the hurdles while a coach throws a basketball to them (Photo 4-4).

It is important to emphasize that jumping drills are *not* to be done on concrete or tile surfaces. Injuries to knees can occur more frequently on concrete or tile as opposed to grassy or wood surfaces.

Photo 4-2

Photo 4-3

Photo 4-4

Stop and Go Running

This exercise can be run using a basketball court or any 15-20 yard straightaway. On the coach's whistle, players sprint until the whistle is blown again, then make a balanced stop, stay low, turn the other way, and sprint in that direction until the next whistle. The coach should make the sprints different lengths to keep the players from anticipating the whistle. The players should stay low and pivot quickly. The coach can gradually increase the duration of the drill.

Slides with Hand/Eye Coordination

This drill requires three small objects that can be picked up and carried while sliding, such as blocks of treated wood or similar items. The coach should place two of these blocks 15-20 feet apart. Players hold the third block in their hand. They should maintain a good defensive stance and slide to one of the blocks on the floor, put their block down and pick up the one from the floor, and slide the other direction, repeating the process. This drill should initially be run for 30 seconds and gradually increased to two minutes. The goal for repetitions should be adjusted based on the age of the players.

Photo 4-5

Photo 4-6

Jump Rope

A jump rope is a valuable tool for helping athletes develop and maintain coordination. When players jump rope, they should not turn the rope by making big sweeping motions with their arms. Instead, they should keep their hands at their waist and turn their wrists to keep the rope going.

A high school senior should be able to do 300 rope jumps in two minutes. A seventh or eighth grader should be able to do 150-200. Coaches should adjust these figures based on the age and conditioning level of their players.

Tire Drill

This drill is similar to the small hurdles drill. Players jump in and out of a tire, jumping with the right foot, left foot, or both feet.

Tire Run Drill

The coach should position 5-12 tires in a line. The players should run quickly down the line, placing one foot in the tires. They should concentrate on keeping their balance and coordination.

Four-Square Tire Drill

The coach should place four tires in a square. Players jump from tire to tire around the square, using the right foot, left foot, and both feet.

Run in Place Drill

This drill is also called the Fast-Feet Drill. Players should get in a good stance with their feet slightly wider than their shoulders and run in place as quickly as they can. This drill should initially be run for 30 seconds and gradually increased to two or three minutes. A coach should also add quick quarter turns to the left and right. These turns should be done on the coach's whistle, with the players making the quick turn and then returning to their original position and continuing the drill.

Wall/Basket Tipping

Players should stand in front of a wall or basket, throw the ball off the wall or backboard, and work on tipping the ball with one hand. Players should work with both the left hand and the right hand. When tipping, the arm should be fully extended and locked at the elbow. The player should use a quick flick of the wrist to tip the ball, land in a balanced position, and go back up to tip the ball again. Players should try to continue tipping the ball for a designated period of time without making a mistake.

Photo 4-7

26

All Fours Drill
Players should get down on all fours in a good, low four-point football stance. They should slide back and forth between two designated spots on the floor as quickly as possible. This drill helps improve agility, coordination, and quickness.

Photo 4-8

Diagonal Rope Drill
The coach should attach a 15-20 foot rope to a wall or door at a height of four feet and anchor the other end to the floor. Players should stand with one side to the rope and, using a two-footed take off, jump quickly from side to side over the rope. They continue to progress up the rope until they do not think they can jump any higher, then turn around and jump backwards down the rope to the starting point, repeating for 30 seconds.

Photo 4-9

Cut and Go Drill

The coach marks the floor with taped X's at various spots. Beginning at one baseline, the players run the length of the floor. They should hit the "X" with the outside foot, plant the foot, and push off it for a quick change of direction. Performing this drill correctly requires concentration and coordination. The coaches should focus on timing and coordination rather than speed during this drill.

Photo 4-10

Body Obstacle Race

This activity is designed to increase foot agility, coordination, and quickness in reaction. The squad is divided into two equal teams. The players lie prone on their backs or on their stomachs in two straight lines as indicated in Diagram 4-1. When the drill is run for the first time, the players should be five to six feet apart. The relay race begins with the first player in each line running and jumping over the players who lie prone on their backs. When the players reach the last player on the floor, they turn around and jump over their teammates again until they reach their original positions. When they reach their original positions they lie back down on the floor and yell "go," which signals the next player in line to repeat the same procedure. The winner is the first team to have all players complete the relay.

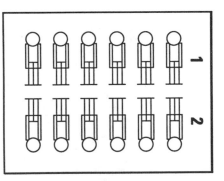

Diagram 4-1

Coaches can vary this drill by increasing or decreasing the distance between players on the floor, making it more difficult to time the jumps properly. They can also require players to use a pull-up jump, taking off from both feet, or run backward over the prone players. All of these variations help increase foot coordination and agility, as well as provide a fun activity for the players.

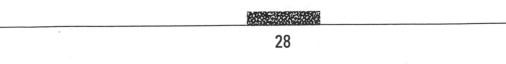

CHAPTER 5

Conditioning

In order to play the game of basketball effectively, players must be able to run up and down the court and change directions quickly. Players who are out of shape will not be able to withstand the rigors of an entire game.

There are so many skills and techniques for players to learn that running alone is not the most efficient use of a coach's limited practice time. Coaches should search for drills that combine conditioning with important basketball skills. The following drills, for example, can be run either as explained or while dribbling a basketball.

Sideline Sprints
The players line up on one sideline and sprint back and forth from sideline to sideline. The goal is to be able to cross the court 14-16 times in one minute.

Full-Court Sprints
This drill is similar to the sideline sprints, but the players line up on one baseline and sprint the length of the court. The goal is to run the length of the court 9-10 times in one minute.

Stop and Go
The kids begin sprinting as hard as they can. When the coach blows the whistle, they stop and begin sprinting in the opposite direction. This continues for 30 seconds to one minute.

Defensive Slides
Players line up at one elbow of the free throw lane and slide back and forth from elbow to elbow for 30 seconds.

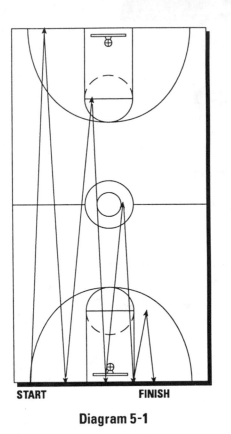

START **FINISH**

Diagram 5-1

Single-Line Touch Drill

All coaches run some variation of this drill. The players start at one baseline. They run and touch the opposite baseline and return to the start, run and touch the opposite free throw line and return to the start, run and touch the 10-second line and return to the start, and run and touch the near free throw line and return to the start.

The coach may vary the drill by requiring the players to run with their arms raised above their shoulders.

Double-Line Touch Drill

This drill is run in the same manner as the Single-Line Touch Drill except that the players run and touch each line twice before moving on to the next one.

Distance Conditioning

Youngsters who are determined to be good basketball players should continue to practice during the off-season. Distance running is a good way for players to stay in shape. The following three programs are recommended for players to use in the off-season or on their own time during the season. Coaches will usually not have time to implement them in their normal practice schedules. It is important to realize that adjustments have to be made for each drill depending on the age and physical maturity level of the players.

Program 1

Cross Country Running

This program involves 30 minutes of running or jogging anywhere. The player runs until fatigued, walks until rested, and runs again. The player continues to run and walk for 30 minutes.

Program 2

Lap Program

A football field works best for this program. Players sprint 40 yards, walk the next 10 yards, and sprint the next 40 yards. They then run backward around the goal post and end zone and repeat the process on the other side of the field.

After completing one lap around the field, the players rest for 30 seconds, then run another lap. Players should try to start out with three or four laps around the field and gradually increase the total number of laps.

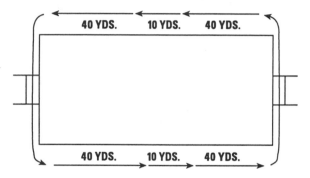

Diagram 5-2

Program 3

Sprint Program

Players should run 10 40-yard sprints, with a 15 second rest after each. They should run each sprint as hard as they can. If it is possible to time them, their goal should be to be between 5.0 and 5.9 seconds for each sprint. This goal may vary based on players' ages and conditioning levels.

CHAPTER 6

Basketball Stance

Players do very little in basketball without first getting into a basketball stance. It is important for them to learn this position because it is the position from which they dribble, jump, pass, catch, slide to defend, and prepare to shoot. The players begin with their feet shoulder-width apart, their backs relatively straight, and their knees flexed. Their knees and shoulders should be pointed straight ahead, not to one side or the other. The players' hands should be held in front of their chests with the palms facing forward and the fingers pointed up, keeping the elbows close to the body. Their heads should be slightly forward and centered over their feet so that a string dropped from the nose would land in the middle of an imaginary line between the feet.

This position is not a natural one. At first it will be difficult for the players and place a lot of stress on the muscles of their thighs. Players need to train the muscles to accept and memorize this stance so they can get into this position quickly on the court whenever it is necessary. During games they will not have time to think about getting into the proper position; therefore, the stance should become second nature to them.

A coach's responsibility is to teach this stance and help the players make it a habit. One of the benefits of using the whistle technique (three short blast of the whistle) to get the players' attention is that it also requires the players to get in their basketball stance. By using this technique five or six times during practice, coaches can help their players become comfortable in this stance.

Fast Feet Drill
This drill is used to develop quickness, agility, and coordination while incorporating the basketball stance. The players form lines with the youngsters positioned two to three feet apart. The commands used in this drill are stance, drive, quick left, quick right, and jump.

Stance: The players get into their basic basketball stance.

Drive: The players run in place as quickly as they can. They should move their feet quickly up and down, only about an inch off the floor, while maintaining their stance. Coaches should make sure the players do not straighten up out of their stance.

Quick Left: The players make a quarter turn to the left, then a quick quarter turn back to their original position, while still running in place. They should maintain their basketball position during the turns. To make the quarter turn effective, the players' feet and shoulders should be square to the left before they return to their original position.

Quick Right: This command is the same as Quick Left except the quarter turn is to the right.

Jump: The players should jump continuously on a "touch and go" basis. As soon as they land, they immediately jump again. They should not take a "gather step" before going back up. Their arms should be raised above the shoulders.

The coach's commands, which are usually given every four to eight seconds, might go something like this: "Stance. Drive. Quick Right. Quick Left. Jump. Drive. Jump. Drive. Quick Right. Quick Left. Stance. Relax." This sequence would last 30-60 seconds, depending on the age and conditioning level of the players. The coach can run the drill just once, or give the players a brief rest period and run it again.

Simon Says Drill
This drill is a second version of the Fast Feet Drill coaches can use to work on agility, coordination, and quickness while teaching players to listen attentively. The drill is based on the game Simon Says, which means players only react to a command when "Simon" says it. A command of "Simon says stance" means that the players get into their basketball stance. A command of "drive" means nothing. Players who react to commands not prefaced by "Simon says" are out of the game.

Triple-Threat Position
The triple-threat position is an important technique for young basketball players to master. Players who use this position are able to keep defenders from playing too close to them, which gives them room to maneuver. If players do not use the triple-threat position, defenders are able to play "belly up" defense on them and keep them from doing anything with the basketball, which gives the advantage to the defense.

When players hold the ball in the triple-threat position, they have three options: they can dribble it, pass it, or shoot it. The stance is the same as the regular basketball stance but the player is holding the basketball. The ball should be cradled in the tuck position, meaning the ball is held in front of the right side of the chest (if the player is right-handed), and may be resting slightly against the chest. The hands are positioned on the ball in such a way that the player can dribble it, pass it to a teammate, or shoot it quickly without having to move the hands.

Photo 6-1

Photo 6-2

The players should have their knees bent, their backs relatively straight, and their heads up looking at the basket. Many players, especially beginners, do not look at the basket when they catch the ball. An offense can not be successful if players do not immediately get into triple-threat position and face the basket when they receive a pass. While holding the ball, players should be able to pivot, or "rock." This movement is called the rocker motion or rocker step. The importance of executing a pivot was mentioned in an earlier chapter. The rocker step is a pivot made while holding the ball in triple-threat position.

Offensive Positioning For the Inside Post Player

Since the post players usually play with their backs to the hoop, they will often receive a pass while facing away from the basket. This positioning means they can not follow the same rules as perimeter players after pass reception: face the basket, tuck the ball, and get in triple-threat position. A different set of positioning techniques applies to the inside post players.

When working with young inside post players, it is important for coaches to remember several points.

First, young inside post players are usually tall and gangly, and often awkward. They generally earn the post position by virtue of being the tallest or heaviest players on the team. Patience is critical in working with the post player. It can take a lot of time and effort to produce results, especially if the post player is not yet as coordinated as other players on the team. The coach and player should learn to work at the right pace for the individual athlete. It is important that the coach utilize drills to help the post player succeed and gain confidence. Drills that are extremely difficult for the player to perform are counterproductive to the important task of building confidence. The players should be able to see their progress.

The post players should understand they are the focal point of the offense. When they get the ball they are the most important player on the court. They should know the offense thoroughly and be able to read defenses. They should also be unselfish and pass the ball back out if they do not have a good shot. This attitude will increase the willingness of other players to pass the ball in to the post.

Post players should be intelligent enough to recognize where and how the defense is playing them. The defender may be playing in one of three ways: in front of, behind, or to the side of the post player. The offensive post players should not determine what move they are going to use until they actually get the ball. They allow the defense to determine how they receive the ball and what they do after they gain possession of it.

Positioning

As the ball is being brought upcourt, post players should line up on the high side of the block and face into the lane. The simple maneuver of facing into the lane can cause problems for the defense. Defenders are not accustomed to having the players they are guarding face them and stare them in the eye, and they may feel uncomfortable playing in front of the post player.

As the ball is brought to the wing area of the court, post players should take their first step toward the baseline to drive their defender down. They then pivot into the defender to seal the defender off. The pivot should be executed properly, with the knees flexed, the hips down, and the arms up with elbows out to take up as much space on the court as possible.

In order to perfect this move, the guards, forwards, and post players should work on their timing every day in practice, initially without any defenders. The forward (F) moves to get open as the guard (G) dribbles across the 10-second line (Diagram 6-1). The post player (C), facing the lane, eyes the guard and initiates the pivot move into the defensive center as the forward pops out to receive the ball.

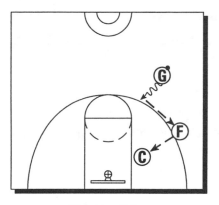

Diagram 6-1

The coach can increase the difficulty of the drill by adding a defender on the offensive guard. This pressure on the guard will disrupt the timing of the play and force the forward and the post player to make adjustments. The coach can then add a second defender on the forward, and finally a third defender on the post player. The post defender should first play behind the offensive post player, then on the baseline side, and then on the high side. The addition of the post defender will allow the coach to begin making adjustments in the offensive post player's positioning.

The type of pass to expect and the shot the post player should use will be covered in detail later. In general, if the defender is playing on the high side, the post player should expect a bounce pass or overhead pass and attempt a power lay-up. If the defender is on the baseline side, or low side, the post player should expect a bounce pass, overhead pass, or halo pass (a quick pass thrown between the so-called "halo" between the defender's head and outstretched arm) and use a hook in the middle.

If the defender is playing behind, the offensive post player should expect a bounce, overhead, or halo pass and use a quick pivot jumpshot or a one-dribble drive move. If the defender is fronting, the post player should expect a lob pass from the forward at the strongside wing, from the guard while swinging into the lane (Diagram 6-2), or from the weakside forward who has flashed across high (Diagram 6-3). On any of the three passes, the post player will use a short jumpshot or power lay-up.

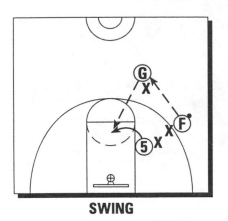

SWING

Diagram 6-2

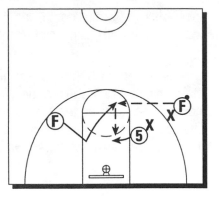

Diagram 6-3

The Target

After learning to read and combat defenses, it is important that post players be taught to want the ball. They will never get the basketball unless they present a good target to the passers. The hand and arm farthest from the defense should be raised high in the air. Players who do not raise their arms will never get a pass.

This rule should be emphasized to other players on the team. No matter what kind of pass is used, post players should first signal the passer with their upraised hand and arm. This signal tells passers that the post player is properly positioned and wants the ball. There may be times when post players do not want the ball because they feel they are not open or are not properly positioned. In those cases, they should keep their target hand and arm down to communicate this feeling to the passer.

The nontarget arm should be positioned in one of two ways. In the first method, the hand is under the chin with the elbow jutting out beyond the plane of the body. This position helps eliminate pushing-off fouls, yet it is effective in warding off defenders, especially if they are playing on the side, because an elbow in the chest is very uncomfortable. When a team has a big, strong post player or a size advantage in the post, this method is very effective.

The second method is often used by smaller post players against bigger opponents. Small post players battling large defenders should take up as much space on the court as they can by establishing a wide base with their legs and knees, raising the target hand, and extending the nontarget arm out away from the body, parallel to the floor. Unfortunately, referees sometimes call offensive fouls against post players using this method. If that situation occurs, the player should switch to the first method described in order to avoid foul trouble.

The Pass

Anticipation and expectation are important concepts to basketball players and teams. Players should be able to anticipate the opponent's moves and expect their teammates to do certain things in certain situations. These skills are learned through concentrated efforts in practice sessions as players observe their teammates' reactions to various situations and learn to read defenses.

Post players should be familiar with their teammates and their passing abilities. Every player should be taught which types of passes should be used in specific situations. Post players can position themselves and prepare to handle passes better if they know what type of pass to expect.

For most players, their passing skills are their weakest area. Players work early and often on their dribbling and shooting skills, but rarely spend any time improving their passing techniques. Coaches who emphasize good passing skills at every practice will be winners.

Teaching passing techniques usually begins with emphasis on the proper form: players should step toward the receiver, keep their knees flexed, and release the ball with the thumbs turned down and the palms facing out. With young players especially, it is good to begin with this method. However, because of the quickness and talent of players today, it is sometimes difficult to always use proper passing form. In these situations, it is most important that the pass reach its intended receiver. The rule in these situations is to pass away from the defense using the best pass to get the ball to its intended receiver.

The best places from which to pass to the post player are the free throw line extended and the top of the key. The most difficult spot from which to feed the post player is the baseline. All players should be taught these concepts. They must understand the game in order to be the best players they can be.

Coaches should also teach players when they should and should not pass. Ballhandlers who are being loosely guarded should not pass the ball. Instead, they should put the ball on the floor, forcing defenders to guard them more tightly. Only when ballhandlers are closely guarded are they in a passing position.

Young players often have difficulty determining when to pass, shoot, and drive. Being able to read the defense and recognize when they are being closely guarded are the keys to passing successfully. It is difficult to pass the ball to its intended receiver when the defender is in a sag position or only loosely guarding the player with the ball.

The basic pass into the post is the bounce pass. Defensive post players often have trouble getting down low enough or quickly enough to intercept this pass. Perimeter players should be encouraged to master and utilize the bounce pass, and post players should learn to expect it. It is important for teams to work on the timing of the guards, forwards, and post players using the bounce pass in practice.

Post players who are being fronted by the defense should be looking for a lob pass from their teammates. Post players being sided on the baseline should expect the bounce pass, halo pass, or overhead flip pass. Players who are being sided on the high side should expect a bounce or overhead pass. If the defense is playing behind post players, they should be looking for the bounce pass.

These rules are basic starting points. There will be times when defenders on either the passer or the post player will force different scenarios. Coaches should first teach all of their players the basic rules, and then teach them how to make appropriate adjustments when necessary.

Catching the Pass

The post player is in the proper position, giving the proper target with the target arm, placing the nontarget arm in a position to ward off the defender without being called for an offensive foul, and reading the defense. The pass is on its way. All the post player has to do is catch the pass to have an easy two points. This task sounds easy, but many players have done all the preparation and then failed to catch the ball because they have not concentrated on this phase of the game. Catching the ball is a critical skill that coaches should emphasize in practice.

When catching the ball, players should lean against the defender, using their hips and thighs to keep the defender at bay. Whenever possible, players should use both hands to catch the ball, with the palms facing the ball. If the palms are facing each other the player is grabbing the ball rather than catching it. Players should not be encouraged to catch the ball with one hand, but it is sometimes necessary and should be covered in practice. If a two-handed catch is not possible, post players should be taught to balance the ball on their wrist, cupping the fingers and palm over the ball when the ball hits their target hand. They should then bring their other hand over the ball in the chest area to protect it. This method is a dangerous way to catch the ball, but coaches should go over it in practice so the post player knows how to do it in a game situation.

Like any other receiver, when sided or played from the rear, post players should come to the pass while giving up as little ground as possible. When fronted, the post players should follow the rules outlined earlier and hold their ground while the pass is in the air. Most important, players should never try to make a move until they have the ball in their hands.

Photo 6-3

Once the pass has been received, it should be brought immediately into the chest area and held next to the chest with the elbows protruding outward (Photo 6-3). The head should be turned quickly toward the baseline, the chin above the shoulder. These two maneuvers, the chesting of the ball and the turning of the head toward the baseline, are preliminary steps to whichever offensive move will follow.

There are many combination drills used to teach post positioning, catching, and passing. Three of the best drills are the Catch and Slide Drill, the Blind Catch Drill, and the Double-Team Post Drill.

Catch and Slide Drill
Players position themselves around the perimeter as shown in Diagram 6-4. The post player must slide and move and is not allowed to leave the multipurpose area until he or she has received a pass from each of the five perimeter players. After receiving a pass from each perimeter player, the post player can make a move to the basket. The defender tries to prevent the passes into the post. If the defender gets a hand on two passes, then the defender and the offensive post player change positions.

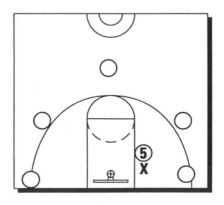

Diagram 6-4

Blind-Catch Drill

This drill is designed to teach the post player to 1) find the ball when it is in the air, 2) handle a pass that is poorly thrown, and 3) make something good out of a bad situation. A coach is the passer in this drill, since a bad pass has to be made. Coaches should never allow players to make bad passes, even in practice drills.

The post player is in a normal position facing the basket. The coach yells, "Now," and the post player executes a quick reverse pivot spin and finds the ball. The coach deliberately throws a poor pass. The post player has to find the ball and move to the basket. To add difficulty to the drill, the coach can decide to add a defensive player on the post player.

Double-Team Post Drill

This drill is designed to teach the post player to catch the ball in a crowd, protect the ball, and then dish it off to an open teammate. The players are positioned as shown in Diagram 6-5.

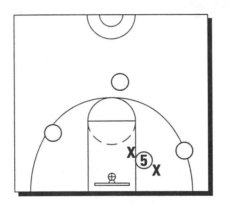

Diagram 6-5

Two defenders are assigned to the post player (#5 in the diagram). No defenders are assigned to the other three offensive players. The ball must be thrown into the post player in the multipurpose area before any shot is taken. The post player receives the ball and then dishes it off to one of the perimeter players, who move to open shooting slots. After the post player has mastered these techniques fairly well, the coach should put a defender on each perimeter player and play four offensive players against five defenders. In this particular phase of the drill, another defender sags on the post player after he or she receives the ball, triple teaming the post. The post player then has to find the open perimeter player.

The Power Dribble

Because of their position near the basket and because they are usually the tallest or strongest players on the court, defenses tend to sag around post players, dropping two or even three defenders to the post. For this reason, post players need to learn a type of dribble different from those used by other players on the team. The high-speed dribble is not appropriate in the post area. Coaches should teach post players one simple dribble: the power dribble.

After post players receive the ball and chest it properly, they should try to make a play using the power dribble. To execute the power dribble (Photo 6-4), post players take a drop step and pound the ball hard off the floor so when they catch the ball, it will be close to the body at about waist level. When the power dribble is performed properly, with the ball thrown hard against the floor, it will come back up so fast that it almost appears as if it never left the player's hands. If post players can learn to coordinate their foot movement with this dribble, they present a formidable offensive threat. The power dribble gives them momentum as they go to the basket. Coaches should also teach post players to never try to dribble the ball away from their body or above the waist unless they have an unimpeded path to the basket.

Dribbling

It is important for players to master the art of dribbling the basketball. Dribbling is a vital part of the game of basketball. Dribbling and dribble moves must be mastered by any individual who wants to develop into a complete player.

Proficient dribblers have several advantages on the court:

1. They can face the defense and see the entire floor.
2. They can eliminate the overly aggressive defender.
3. They can back up in traffic and maintain their poise.

General Components

Dribblers should assume a good balanced body position: head up, chin parallel to the ground, feet shoulder width apart, and knees bent to keep the body low. The fingers of the dribble hand should be spread comfortably with the hands slightly cupped to give good ball control. The wrist of the dribble hand does the majority of the work and the elbow of the dribble arm is kept close to the body to eliminate upper arm motion. The dribble itself should be kept relatively low—no higher than the waist— and should hit the floor in front and slightly outside of the feet. The ball should be dribbled hard. The harder the dribble, the quicker the ball returns to the hand and the quicker the dribbler can move. Players should train themselves not to look down at the ball. By putting their head own, dribblers isolate themselves from the rest of the team. They will not see cutters, open shooters, or defenders coming up to steal the ball.

There are basically two types of dribbles: the low-protective dribble and the high-speed dribble.

Low-Protective Dribble

In the low-protective dribble, the dribbler is balanced at the knees and the waist. When players are excellent dribblers, it is hard to see their hand separate from the ball. Players should protect the ball with their body in basic basketball position, keeping their body between the ball and the defender.

Photo 7-1

Players should pump the ball downward and, as they make contact, flick the wrist. They have to make sure they hit the ball hard enough to come back up when it hits the floor. Their hand should stay with the ball. Good dribblers put their hands on the side of the ball. This technique is difficult for beginners, but as players improve, they can use the side of the ball to guide it better, to fake better, and to better keep the defense honest and away from them.

Protecting in a Rectangle

Coaches should mark a rectangle on the floor with tape, approximately two feet by one and a half feet. One player dribbles the ball and another tries to steal it. The dribbler must stay in the rectangle. This drill teaches players to protect the ball in a small, confined area by keeping their body between the ball and the defender.

Photo 7-2

Dribble Tag

The coach should divide the team into pairs. The first pair is given basketballs and instructed to dribble in the three-second lane while trying to knock the other player's basketball away. This drill forces the players to stay down in a low, protective dribble stance, while keeping the head up to see where the other player is.

As the players get better with the low protective dribble coaches can place three, four, or even five players in the lane dribbling basketballs and trying to knock the ball away from their teammates. Once a ball is knocked out of the lane, that player is eliminated. The one player left dribbling is the winner.

Photo 7-3

High-Speed Dribble

The second dribble that must be mastered by every basketball player is the high-speed dribble. This dribble is different from the low-protective dribble because the dribbler is trying to explode past the defense and either drive to the basket or get an open shot. The dribble must be higher and harder than the low-protective dribble simply because the player is moving quickly past the defense, trying to escape the defender.

Players should dribble the ball waist high or slightly higher, and put it out in front of them and to the side so they will not kick it as they increase their speed. The coach should watch all the players on the squad to make sure they are dribbling the ball correctly.

Photo 7-4

Sideline High-Speed Drill

Each player is given a basketball and lined up along the sideline or a taped line on the court with both feet on the left side of the line. The players dribble the basketball on the right side of the line, first walking, then jogging, then going full speed. This drill enables the coach to look right down the line and see which players are not putting the ball out in front and to the side. If the ball is not dribbled out in front and to the side on the high-speed dribble, the player will probably either outrun the ball or kick it.

Photo 7-5

Next, the players start with both feet on the right side of the sideline and dribble the ball on the left side of the line with the left hand. Players should dribble while standing, then walking, then jogging, then sprinting. Again, coaches should emphasize that the ball should be slightly out in front and to the side of the player.

Another drill that can be used to teach the high-speed dribble is the full-court dribbling drill, in which the player dribbles down the court with the right hand and returns using the left.

An excellent combination drill to teach both the low-protective and high-speed dribble is the circle drill.

Circle Drill

Players line up under the basket, each with a ball. They should use the high-speed dribble everywhere except when going around the circle. When dribbling around the three circles, the player should slow down and glide around the circle using the low-protective dribble. When the players reach the other end of the court and come around that circle for the last time, they explode to the basket with a high-speed dribble and shoot a lay-up.

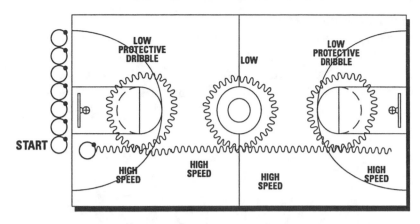

Diagram 7-1

Putting the Hand on the Side of the Ball

Most youngsters think that they are only allowed to dribble with their hand on top of the ball. It is illegal for players to put their hand underneath the ball and cup the ball as they dribble it. This maneuver is called carrying the basketball. However, it is legal for players to put their hand on the side of the ball. Most good dribblers do this, and do it quite efficiently. The following drills help a youngster learn the technique of placing the hand on the side of the ball.

Using just the right hand, players stand in basketball position and dribble the ball from side to side in front of their body. Players then

Photo 7-6

dribble side to side on the right side of their body, then between the legs and around the back. Using only the right hand forces players to put their hand on the side of the ball in order to go between their legs, around their back, or from side to side. The drill is then repeated using only the left hand.

Mastering Other Dribble Moves

There are many dribble moves youngsters can practice and eventually master, including the crossover, the around the back dribble, the between the legs dribble, the reverse spin, and the fake reverse spin. For their first year or two, young players should work primarily on the low-protective and high-speed dribbles. After players have mastered these two, they may work on the fancy dribbles.

Photo 7-7

The On-Side Dribble

The first dribble move that should follow the low-protective and high-speed dribble is the on-side dribble. The ball is dribbled with the right hand while the dribbler is facing the defender. The dribbler then fakes everything—head, shoulder, and foot—to the left, but keeps the ball to the right. As the defender reacts to the fake left, the dribbler explodes by on the right side toward the basket.

Photo 7-8

The best way to teach the on-side dribble is to mark off a rectangle with tape for each player. The player stands in the rectangle and begins to dribble the ball outside the rectangle with the right hand. Upon the coach's command of "fake," the player fakes left with the head, shoulder, and foot while keeping the ball to the right.

The next step in the teaching process is to have players walk while dribbling the basketball. The coach places a chair 25-30 feet out on the court. When the players reach the chair, they execute the on-side fake to the left and explode by the chair on the right.

Coaches can vary the drill by placing several chairs on the court for players to fake at or by having players dribble with their left hand so they fake right and explode by on the left.

Final Pointers on the On-Side Dribble
As dribblers execute the fakes in one direction, they have a tendency to get off balance. Raising the dribble slightly will enable players to maintain their balance.

If players become proficient with the on-side dribble, they can next learn to bring the basketball slightly to the left, while faking left, by placing the right hand on the left side of the ball as if going left. They then quickly switch the hand to the right side of the ball, moving it back to the right. This technique is especially effective because many defenders watch the basketball. Moving the ball first to the left and then quickly back to the right improves the player's chance of escaping the defender. This maneuver is extremely difficult, and should be practiced only after mastering the basic techniques.

A Ballhandling Program for Individual Workouts
Everyone can learn to handle the basketball. It takes about 10 minutes a day with each hand to master the skill. Size and age are not factors. All youngsters can learn to handle the basketball. If a normal basketball is too big, players can use a junior-sized ball, a mini basketball, or even a tennis ball.

Ballhandling
Players should stand in place with their feet parallel and dribble the ball outside their right leg. They should pound the ball hard, with a wrist snap and arm pumping motion, not slap at the ball.

Players should first dribble for five minutes with the right hand, and then five minutes with the left hand. They should then put their left hand behind their back and dribble the ball between their legs, from side to side, and in front using only the right hand. To accomplish this, they have to learn to put their hand on the side of the ball to dribble it, rather than just putting their hand on top of the ball. They players should then repeat the drill, using their left hand while keeping their right hand behind their back.

Crossover Drill

As players become more proficient with their dribbles they can add various dribble moves. They should start with the high-speed dribble and the on-side dribble and then add others. Another type of dribble is the crossover dribble. The ball should go from one side of the body to the other, bouncing in front of and close to the body. This move is dangerous because the change is directly in front of the defender. If players put the ball on the floor too far from their bodies, the defender will steal it.

Around the Back

It is helpful for players to be proficient at several dribbles. Players who can successfully dribble the ball around their back will be able to escape certain situations and become more valuable to their team. The around the back dribble is more difficult to master than the crossover. Players should keep their bodies in front of the defender as the ball comes around the back.

Between the Legs

Players can practice this dribble by standing alone and continuously repeating it. They should not lift their legs on this dribble. The leg protects the ball, while it is going from one hand to the other.

Dribble Drill

Players should begin about 30 feet from the basket. They dribble down one side and shoot the lay-up, then dribble directly out to the other side and repeat, using the other hand. They should practice one type of dribble at a time.

High-speed dribble: two minutes

On-side dribble: two minutes

Crossover dribble: two minutes

Fancy dribble (around the back or between the legs): two minutes

CHAPTER 8

Passing and Catching

Passing is probably the aspect of basketball worked on the least by coaches and by players. Not only are the fundamentals of passing important, but players should be taught when they should pass rather than dribble or shoot. Players should also understand that passing advances the basketball more quickly than the dribble does.

Besides passing and catching, coaches should also teach their players how to fake.

Rules for Faking:
- If players are being closely guarded and wish to pass the ball low (the bounce pass), they should fake high.
- If players are being closely guarded and wish to pass the ball high, they should fake the bounce pass low.
- If players wish to pass left, they should fake and look right.
- If players wish to pass right, they should fake and look left.

Before teaching youngsters how to pass the basketball, it is important for coaches to determine whether they know how to catch the basketball.

Techniques for Catching
When catching the ball, players should open the palms and have them facing the passer. They should spread their fingers evenly, creating a larger surface to receive the ball. The thumbs should be six- to eight-inches apart. The receiver should always step toward the incoming pass, catch it with the arms extended, and then draw the ball inward to the chest. The player then pivots, faces the basket, and gets into triple-threat position.

Good Hands Drills
These drills help young players become better receivers.

Pound Drill
Players take a basketball and pound it back and forth between their hands. They should do this as hard as they can to toughen up their hands.

Two-Man Passing Drill

This drill is effective in teaching both passing and receiving. The team is divided into pairs. The partners pass the ball back and forth, concentrating on a specific pass—chest pass, bounce pass, or overhead pass. Passers should bend their knees and step toward the receiver, passing the ball to the outside hand. Receivers should step toward the ball and the passer. Most passes should arrive between the receiver's waist and chest.

Over the Shoulder Toss

Players hold the ball out in front of the right shoulder at shoulder height. They then toss the ball directly over the right shoulder and try to catch it with both hands behind their back (Photo 8-1). As soon as the fingers feel the ball, they should squeeze and hold it. The drill is not effective if the ball is tossed in such a way that players arch their back and let the ball roll down the back.

Photo 8-1

Blind-Catch Drill

Players stand at the block with their back to the coach, who has assumed a position on the wing. Players should be in a good basketball position with their hands ready in front of their chest. When the coach yells "Now," the players execute a quick 180-degree jump turn, landing in a balanced position with their feet and shoulders squared to the coach, who makes the pass. The receivers catch the ball, draw it to their chest, and execute a lay-up at the basket.

The coach can vary the timing of the pass depending upon the athletic ability of the player. Passing the ball while the jump turn is being executed will force the player to really concentrate on the fundamentals of catching. Passing the ball a split second before the player jump turns also improves catching agility, coordination, quickness, and balance. Many younger players are scared of this drill because they do not want the ball to hit them. The coach should take the time to reassure them and remind them that if their hands are properly aligned in front of their chest, palms facing forward with the thumbs about eight inches apart, the ball will hit their hands. With practice, they will learn to catch it.

Jump and Catch Drill

The coach should place obstacles such as cones or small hurdles on the floor. As players jump over the obstacles, the coach makes a chest pass to them. Players should execute the jump, watch the pass, catch the ball on the floor or while airborne, and return it to the coach with a good chest pass.

Backboard Blind Catch Drill

Players stand about 8-10 feet in front of the rim with their backs to the basket, facing the coach, who is standing at the free throw line. The coach yells "Now" and fires the ball off the backboard as the player executes a quick jump turn. Players should catch the ball off the board and then shoot a lay-up. The coach should assess the athletic ability of each player to determine how hard and high the pass off the backboard will be.

Competitive Passing Drills
Bull in the Ring

Three players are positioned around the circle as shown in Diagram 8-1. A defensive player tries to deflect the basketball as it is passed among the three players. The three offensive players are required to stay in triple-threat position; use short, crisp pass fakes; and use bounce, chest, and overhead passes. If the offensive players have to move from their position to catch a pass, then it is considered a bad pass and the player who made the pass must take the defender's place. If the defender deflects a pass, the person who made the pass becomes the defender.

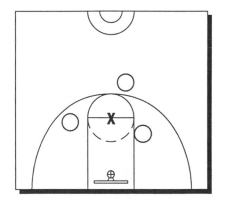

Diagram 8-1

No-Touch Passing Drill

This drill combines the ideas of guarding the basket and challenging the ballhandler to deflect a pass. It forces the defender to make a quick judgment and then react. Players are aligned as shown in Diagram 8-2, with guards in a line near half court and defenders positioned outside the baseline. The guards dribble into the top of the circle area. As soon as they enter this area (the shaded area in the diagram), the defender can challenge the ball. The ballhandler must stop between the top of the key and the free throw line and is challenged by the defender in this area. All the defender must do to be successful is touch the ball. Once the defender touches the ball, the next player in each line steps into the drill.

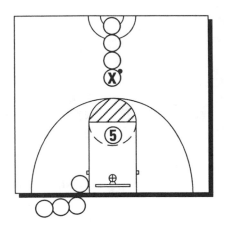

Diagram 8-2

The defender may fake at the dribbler and fake back to play the other offensive player stationed at the block. That offensive player cannot move from the spot. In this situation, the dribbler can either shoot or attempt a quick pass to the player on the block, and the defender reacts appropriately. The drill encourages quick thinking, quick feet, quick hands, and quick reactions on the part of the defender, as well as good passing judgment and techniques.

Two-Ball Passing Drill

This drill focuses on coordination, agility, timing, and spacing. Players should line up as shown in Diagram 8-3 with partners facing each other and each player holding a basketball. Partners should pass the ball to each other simultaneously. Theoretically, the two balls should pass each other at the same time. The players should concentrate on catching the pass and returning it. The players should present a target chest high on their left side (if right-handed). Both players must pass with the same hand for this drill to work. Passers should aim at and hit the target. The coach will designate the type of pass to be made. Timing and concentration are essential. Players should catch the pass in the left hand, clasp the right hand over the ball, swing the ball to the right side, and return the pass. They should begin the drill slowly and increase their speed as they gain confidence.

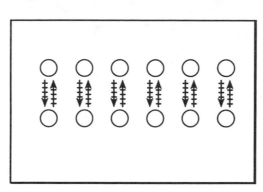

Diagram 8-3

Photo 8-2

Two-Man Full-Court Passing Drill

This drill emphasizes coordination, agility, timing, and spacing. Players form two lines behind one baseline on either side of the free throw lane. Each pair of players has a basketball. They run a two-man fast break to the other end, focusing on spacing and timing, and shoot a lay-up off a bounce pass. After each player has shot a lay-up, the players repeat the drill, shooting a jumpshot from the elbow of the lane, and finally run the drill shooting a bank jumpshot from 8-10 feet.

The player with the ball should stop near or inside the three-point line to spread the defense and create good spacing for the bounce pass. The coach may also choose to add a defender and run a two-on-one fast break.

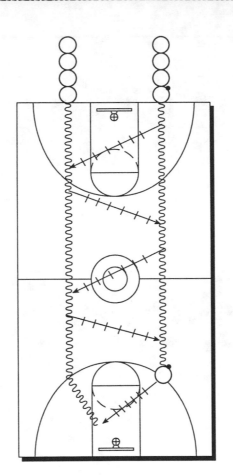

Diagram 8-4

Considerations for Creating Better Passers
- Do the players know how to catch a ball? Their palms should be open, the palms facing the passer, the fingers spread to create a wide target for the ball. They should step to the ball, catch it with their arms extended, and then draw it back toward their chest.
- Timing and spacing are essential to good passing. The pass should be made when the receiver is open and ready to catch it.
- Coaches should teach and develop these concepts of good timing and spacing. For example, the coach can mark spots on the floor as illustrated in Diagram 8-5 and run timing drills. When player #1 reaches a designated spot, player #2 pops out to the second spot for a pass (Diagram 8-6). The coach can then add a third player (Diagram 8-7). Player #1 reaches the designated spot and passes to player #2. Player #4 then goes to his or her spot to receive a pass.

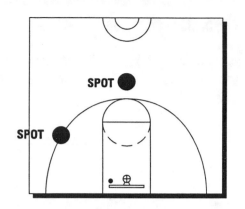

Diagram 8-5

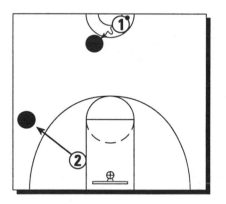

Diagram 8-6

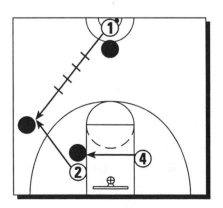

Diagram 8-7

Variations to the Timing Drills
Point-Wing Timing

The point player passes to the wing, fakes to the weakside, and then makes a V-cut down the side of the lane for a return pass (usually a bounce pass) and the lay-up (Diagram 8-8).

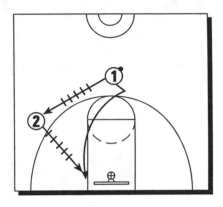

Diagram 8-8

Wing-Post Timing

The wing player passes to the post, then cuts to the baseline or the middle for a short return bounce pass. The coach may also choose to have the wing pass to the post, slide to the baseline for a return pass, and then either take the shot or pass back into the post (Diagram 8-9).

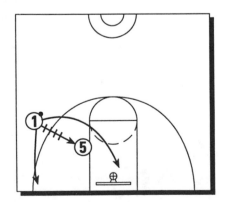

Diagram 8-9

Two timing drill options for four players are illustrated in Diagrams 8-10, 8-11, and 8-12. The point player passes to the strongside wing (Diagram 8-10) and cuts to the baseline. The weakside wing moves to the top of the key. The strongside wing has two options. He or she may pass to player #3, who then passes to the post player cutting across the lane (Diagram 8-11). The strongside wing may also make a return pass to the point player who has cut to the baseline, then fake to the elbow of the lane and make a V-cut around the post player to the block (Diagram 8-12).

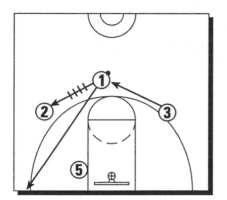

Diagram 8-10

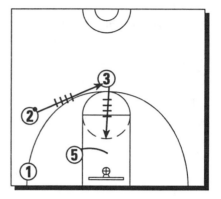

Diagram 8-11

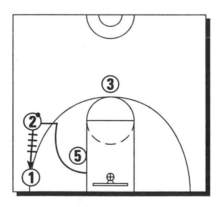

Diagram 8-12

Passing Drills Without Dribbling
In order to emphasize the importance of passing in the game of basketball, coaches can set up games in practice in which the players are not allowed to dribble the ball. For example, the coach may have players compete two-on-two and require them to move the ball using passes, fakes, and cuts rather than the dribble.

For younger players, coaches can require the offense to make a designated number of consecutive, completed passes to gain points; for example, if the offense completes three passes without the defense touching the ball, they earn a point. The coach may also award points for completing passes to specific areas, such as the post area. The coach may also have players work three-on-three without dribbling and teach them to screen away from the ball to get players open. Once the players have grasped the importance of passing the ball, the coach can allow them to attempt to score a basket without dribbling. This type of drill forces players to pass, move, cut, and protect the ball, and can be played two-on-two, three-on-three, four-on-four, or five-on-five. Especially when performing the drill with larger numbers, the coach should insist on proper spacing to keep players from congregating in one small area of the court.

In trying to create proper spacing, cutting and movement along with good passing concept, place 5 X's with tape as shown in Diagram 8-13.

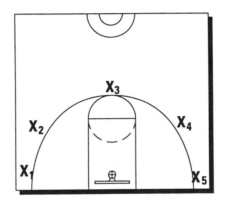

Diagram 8-13

Three players are put on the court, on X3, X4, and X2. Start the player at X3 with the basketball. When X3 passes the ball to either X4 or X2, he or she cuts to another open X on the court—an X that is unoccupied by another player. When a player receives a pass (on an X), he or she faces the basket and gets into triple-threat position, holding the ball for at least two seconds. The other players are moving to another X on the court. This movement continues for a couple of minutes until the coach stops the action. The rules for movement are simple:

- No two players can occupy the same X at the same time.
- All cutters should always look at the person with the ball so that a possible return pass can be made to that particular cutter.

- When passing players can never skip over an X For example, X2 can pass to X1 or X3, but not to X5. X5 can only pass to X4; X3 could pass to spot X2 or X4.

This drill creates excellent movement and cutting with proper spacing between players. Too often kids do *not* understand the concept of proper spacing—staying 12-15 feet away from teammates. This drill also emphasizes conditioning and triple-threat position, along with passing and catching. The coach should make all players pass the ball to the outside hand of their teammates. The coach can also teach screening away from the ball. Later, coaches can allow the players to use the dribble to get from one spot to another or to use the dribble to balance out the floor or to help create timing. When satisfied that their players have mastered all of these techniques, coaches can allow the players to shoot the ball off the movement. In reality, what the coach has done is to create the basis for a half-court offense.

Shooting

Shooting the basketball is the fun part of the game. It is something every player likes to do, but it is also the skill that is most often practiced and developed in the wrong way. Players then have a difficult time breaking these bad habits later.

Four Things That Make a Good Shooter

l. Correct Form and Technique
Though it is very difficult for younger players to develop the correct form in its entirety, there are certain fundamentals that need to be practiced repeatedly to develop muscle memory reflex.

2. Hours of Practice
The correct technique does not do a player any good without many hours of practice. Ten minutes a day is not sufficient. Becoming a good shooter requires one to two hours of perfect practice every day, especially during the off-season.

3. The Right Mental Approach
The right mental approach includes understanding and concentrating on the correct techniques, staying out of the habit of missing, setting goals at every workout and practicing until those goals have been reached, relaxing and having fun, not getting discouraged, and sticking to a practice schedule. Players must make that commitment.

4. Accountability
Players should make themselves accountable for each shot they take. They should know how many they make and how many they miss, and record their shots daily. They should not take shots and miss constantly, take shots they know are not "game shots," or take shots they know they can not make. It is easy for the brain to accept missing; players should not allow themselves to get into this habit.

Correct Form and Technique

Every youngster has two major sources of power with which to shoot the ball: the arms and the legs. Using these sources of power in coordination with each other is very important in propelling the ball toward the basket. A player's strength, age, and size usually determine how much the arms and the legs must be used when shooting the basketball.

Younger, smaller players usually have to bend the knees deeply and lower the ball almost to their ankles in order to get it to the basket (Photos 9-1 through 9-3). These players are utilizing both sources of power available to them, which is the correct technique for shooting the basketball at their age. As players get older, stronger, and bigger, they will be able to focus on the other techniques of shooting and rely less on leg bend and arm movement.

The first step in shooting the basketball is to catch the ball or pick the ball up off the dribble in a bent knee position. The legs supply the power, and in a sense, start the shot.

Photo 9-1

Photo 9-2

Photo 9-3

Stance

When preparing to shoot, the feet and shoulders should be squared to the basket (Photo 9-4). Although in game situations squaring up to the basket is not always possible, it is important that players square to the basket and use the proper techniques when practicing. The shooting foot should be slightly in front of the other. The ball should be held in the tuck position at or near the waist or chest.

Photo 9-4

Head

The head should remain still with the eyes on the target. Players should find a spot, whether it is the front or back of the rim or the entire basket, and focus on that spot for the entire shot. They should repeat this every single time, using the same spot. Players should not let the shooting arm and ball block their vision, making them a one-eyed shooter (Photo 9-5), but position themselves so they can focus on the target with both eyes (Photo 9-6).

Photo 9-5

Photo 9-6

It is acceptable for players to jump a bit on their shot, but they should not jump too much. They should not drift to one side or the other, jump inward, or fall back. This motion is unnecessary and will cause shooters to lose their balance and consequently throw off the shot. When shooting the basketball, less body motion improves the shooter's chance of success. Players should land in relatively the same spot from which they took off, perhaps slightly forward.

Grip

The grip of the hands on the basketball is a crucial element of the shot. Kids should learn to be one-handed shooters rather than two-handed shooters.

Photo 9-7

The index and middle fingers of the shooting hand, the ones which propels the ball, should be in the middle of the ball. The valve can be used as a guide. Players should position the valve between the index and middle finger and spread the other fingers out evenly on the ball (Photo 9-7). This technique will ensure that the hand is in the middle of the ball, creating a good balanced grip. If players can see their little finger on the ball, their grip is wrong; shooters should "hide the pinkie."

Photo 9-8

The widest distance between fingers on the ball is between the thumb and the index finger. The ball should rest not in the palm of the shooting hand, but on the pads of the hands between the fingers and the palm. There should be enough space between the shooting hand and the ball to allow the coach to slip a pencil between the ball and the palm (Photo 9-8).

The non-shooting hand is referred to as the off hand, guide hand, or balance hand. Shooting is essentially a one-handed act. Shooters should not use the off hand to propel the ball, but simply to balance it. The fingers of the guide hand should point to the ceiling. The thumb of the guide hand should point to the shooter's ear. The thumbs should form a "T" on the basketball, but should not be touching each other (Photo 9-9).

Most basketball coaches would agree that there are specific fundamentals to gripping the basketball. Most experts would also agree that there are differences that every coach teaches and advocates. Adjustments also have to be made for players who are smaller or weaker or have small hands. Making these adjustments is an important part of a coach's job.

Photo 9-9

When picking the ball up off the dribble, players should be sure to get the proper grip to shoot. The hands must slide to these positions automatically. Repetition is the only way to ensure this action. Players can flip the ball from hand to hand and practice catching it with the proper grip even when they are not at practice or on a basketball court.

The Release

As a player brings the basketball up to shoot, the ball should be placed above the right eye (for a right-handed shooter) just outside of the head, allowing both eyes to see the target. The elbow keeps the ball straight and it should be tucked to the side and pointed at the basket. The upper arm should be parallel to the floor, with the forearm perpendicular to the floor (Photo 9-10).

Photo 9-10

The arm should form the letter "L" under the ball. The ball should rest over the elbow, and the elbow should be over the shooting foot. The guide hand elbow should be outside of the back foot. The wrist of the shooting hand should be cocked (flexed). If the wrist is cocked properly, the shooter will see wrinkles in the wrist. The release of the shot is extremely important. The initial movement to start the shot is upward. Players should remember to push the ball up, not out. If the release is properly executed, the elbow will end up higher than the chin (Photo 9-12).

Photo 9-11

Photo 9-12

The top of the wrist should be as high as or higher than the backboard. The shot rolls off the index and middle fingers. These two fingers should be the last things to touch the basketball. This technique puts the proper backspin on the ball, creating a softness to the shot. The off hand should come off the ball quickly, with the fingers pointing to the ceiling and the thumb to the ear (Photo 9-13).

Follow-Through

On the follow-through, the fingers of the shooting hand should appear to be cupped slightly over the rim, not pointing to the floor (Photos 9-14 and 9-15). Some coaches use the phrase "Pose for the picture" to remind shooters of this technique.

Photo 9-13

Photo 9-14

Photo 9-15

The arc on the shot is based on several factors, including the shooter's distance from the basket, the use of the backboard, and what is comfortable for the shooter. With too much arc, the shooter may be expending too much energy. Without enough arc, the shot will be too flat. When a shooter is using the backboard on a shot, the ball should be shot higher and softer. An uncoordinated follow-through or no follow-through at all violates the rules of good shooting.

Rules of Good Shooting
1. The body should remain relatively still.
2. The shot should be smooth and balanced.
3. The shooter should concentrate on the proper techniques.
4. The shooter should "pose for the picture" on the follow-through.

Summary of the Techniques of Shooting
One of a coach's responsibilities is to correct poor techniques and help players progress. To fulfill this responsibility, coaches should be aware of the correct techniques and watch the players closely. The shooting checklist on the next page summarizes the techniques of good shooting. Coaches and players should use this list to evaluate a player's development. Videotaping a player's shot for the coach and player to watch together can be very helpful in this evaluation.

Developing Correct Shooting
Warm Up Properly
Coaches should have one ball for every player. Girls and smaller boys can use a girls' ball. Very young players should use a junior-sized ball. Players should learn with a ball that is appropriate for their size.

Rich Grawer Basketball Shooting Checklist

Needs Work — **Triple-Threat Position**
- ☐ 1. Tuck Ball
- ☐ 2. Starting Blocks— knees bent
- ☐ 3. Ball Fakes
- ☐ 4. Ball quick
- ☐ 5. Body to body drives

Needs Work — **Set up**
- ☐ 1. Knees bent
- ☐ 2. 1-2 step approach off pass
- ☐ 3. Squared to basket
- ☐ 4. Off dribble-plant inside foot

Needs Work — **Head and Eyes**
- ☐ 1. Head Still
- ☐ 2. Both eyes on target
- ☐ 3. Don't follow flight of ball

The Grip

Needs Work — **1. Shooting Hand**
- ☐ —hand on the ball, fingers spread
- ☐ —ball on pads
- ☐ —hand in middle of ball

2. Guide Hand/Balance Hand
- ☐ —fingers-pointing to ceiling
- ☐ —thumb to ear
- ☐ —both thumbs form "T"

The Actual Shot and Finish

Needs Work — **1. Elbow and Arm**
- ☐ —elbow tucked to side- pointed at hoop
- ☐ —upper arm parallel to floor
- ☐ —forearm perpendicular to floor
- ☐ —ball over elbow, elbow over shooting foot
- ☐ —guide hand elbow— outside of foot

2. Wrist
- ☐ —cocked (flexed)—see wrinkles

3. Release
- ☐ —extension of arm-push out
- ☐ —roll ball off index and middle finger-backspin
- ☐ —follow thru: wrist as high or higher than backboard; fingers cupped over rim; fingers NOT pointed to floor; pose for picture at least 1 second
- ☐ —follow thru: guide hand gets off ball quickly; fingers of guide hand point to ceiling

4. Jump
- ☐ —land in relatively same spot as left the floor from

Overall Evaluation

On Your Back Shooting Drill

This drill may be performed without a basket or a court. Players lie on their backs on the floor with the ball in their shooting hand. They "shoot" the ball using their normal shooting movement, keeping the elbow close to the body and the seams of the ball horizontal. This positioning helps create backspin on the shot, but most important, it helps players work on their follow-through. As players shoot, they should keep the follow-through position until just before the ball hits their wrist on its way down.

It is easy for players to evaluate themselves when executing this drill. If the ball returns straight to the palm of the hand after the shot, the "shot" was made. If it does not, the "shot" was missed.

Photo 9-16

Chair Drill

The purpose of this drill is to work on getting power from the arms, putting the proper arc on the shot, aligning the elbow correctly, and following through.

The coach should place a chair five to eight feet in front of the basket, depending on the size and strength of the players. The first player sits on the chair. The player must now use his or her arms—not legs—to propel the ball upward to the basket. Players—particularly smaller ones—must start the ball head high and with one rhythmic motion, rotate the arm down to the waist and then back into shooting position to shoot the ball up at the basket. Again, this chair drill forces players to get their arms into the shot.

Photo 9-17

Lay-Ups

The lay-up is the one shot in basketball that determines the outcome of most games. It is also a shot that players and coaches often do not spend much time practicing. Lay-ups include driving shots at the basket, rebounds off missed shots, and short inside shots from the block. These shots should be worked on every day.

Lay-Up Drills

- Players should stand on one side of the basket and shoot lay-ups from that spot. They should raise their outside leg in the air with the thigh parallel to the floor (Photo 9-18). The coach should make sure the shooter is at the proper angle and remains an appropriate distance from the basket. Players should make sure they use the backboard on all shots. After making a designated number of lay-ups from one side of the basket, shooters switch to the other side.

Photo 9-18

- The players move back a step and take two-step lay-ups. On the right side of the basket, players step with their right foot and then their left, pushing off the left foot and raising the right leg so the thigh is parallel to the floor. Players should remember to jump vertically and use the backboard. After making a designated number of shots, players switch to the other side of the basket.

- Players move back another step and take three-step shots, stepping with the left foot, then the right, and then stepping with and jumping off the left foot.

- Players take one high-speed dribble before shooting the lay-up.

- Players take two high-speed dribbles before taking the lay-up.

- Players drive in from half court and shoot the lay-up.

On all of these drills, coaches should make sure players are shooting from the proper distance and at the proper angle.

Lay-Up Contest

Players are given one minute to make as many lay-ups as they can. Younger players are allowed to stay on one side of the basket. Older players must alternate sides on each shot, but may use either hand. Although many players view the contest as a fun part of practice, they are still practicing their lay-ups. Coaches should still be careful to emphasize proper technique.

Drills to Improve Techniques

In order to develop the right grip and follow-through techniques, the coach can wrap a piece of white adhesive tape around the center of the basketball. Players grip the ball with their index and middle fingers straddling the tape. If the players use the correct techniques when shooting, the ball should go toward the basket with proper backspin and the tape on the basketball should rotate symmetrically (Photos 9-19 and 9-20). If the tape "wobbles" or does not rotate at all, there is a flaw in the grip, the release, or the follow-through.

Photo 9-19

Photo 9-20

Another drill helps players grip the ball properly as well as get into proper triple-threat position. Players toss the ball five to six feet in front of them with backspin, then run up and catch it off the bounce, quickly adjusting the hands to the tape on the ball to ensure the proper grip. After catching the ball, players get into triple-threat position and work on rocker steps, fakes, and pivots.

Next, players toss the ball out in front of them, catch it on a balanced jump stop, grip it properly, and take a shot. Players can judge their techniques by watching the rotation of the tape on the ball on its way to the basket.

These "tape on the ball" drills can be used to emphasize the three S's:

- Spin (backspin)
- Stop (players should stop on balance and squared to the basket)
- Sight

While performing drills, coaches should instruct players to work quickly, but not rush themselves. Young kids tend to do things in a hurry. In basketball, this tendency causes players to be off-balance and out of control.

Shooting Off the Dribble

When shooting off the dribble, players should escape their defender and get a good look at the basket. If a defender is close enough to the ballhandler to get a hand in and distract the shooter, the offensive player should not be looking to shoot. When closely guarded, offensive players should look to drive or pass. When players are within their shooting range and are not closely guarded, they should look to shoot or pass.

When shooting off the dribble, players should use the following techniques:

- After getting by the defender, players should come to a jump stop off a hard dribble by planting the inside foot (the one closest to the basket), and swinging the other foot to square to the basket and gain balance. The last dribble before going into the shot should be slightly lower and harder than the others. This gives shooters some momentum as they prepare to jump into the shot.
- The knees should stay bent as the players come to a jump stop.
- While squared to the basket, players should begin their shot using correct form and technique (Photo 9-21).

It is important that each player be able to effectively handle the basketball. Players who can not handle the basketball and escape their defender to get a good shot are very limited in their ability to help their team. Players should work on their ballhandling skills daily; these skills can be practiced without a basket or a court.

Photo 9-21

Shooting Off the Dribble Drills
- Players should form a line at the wing position. Players drive to the middle using two dribbles and take a shot from the free throw line area (Diagram 9-1).

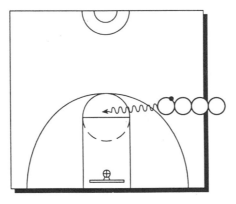

Diagram 9-1

- Players form a line at the top of the key. Players fake right and drive left using one or two dribbles, then shoot. On the second repetition of the drill, players fake left and drive right.

Coaches should pay close attention to the players' techniques during these drills and make corrections when necessary. Above all, coaches should make sure that players cover from 4-6 feet with every dribble of the basketball. Too often, players bounce the ball and cover only 6 to 12 inches of the floor space.

Shooting Under-Pressure Drills
Under-Pressure Drill
The players are aligned as shown in Diagram 9-2, with one defender (X) positioned under the basket and one offensive player (O) at the top of the key. The defender passes out to the offensive player. Offensive players should use a one to two step approach to catch the ball and begin their shot. Defenders rush out at the offensive players and try to distract them as they shoot. The defender is not allowed to touch the ball or the shooter. After the shot is taken, the players go to the end of the opposite line. Coaches should emphasize to their players that good shooters do not allow themselves to be distracted by the defense.

Distract the Player Drill
This drill involves several important basketball techniques. The players are aligned around the arc as shown in Diagram 9-3. The distance from the basket may be adjusted for younger players. X1, the defender, passes the ball out to O7, then rushes out to distract him or her. The defender is not allowed to touch the ball or the shooter. After O7 shoots the ball, X1 takes his or her place. O7 retrieves the ball whether the shot was made or missed and shoots a lay-up. Shooters can earn up to three points. They earn two for a made outside shot and one for a successful lay-up. If the defender touches the ball or the shooter, the shooter is automatically awarded three points and can earn a fourth by making the lay-up. After shooting the lay-up, O7 becomes the defensive player and passes the ball out to the next shooter, O6 in the diagram. The process continues around the arc for a designated number of repetitions, and the player with the most points is the winner.

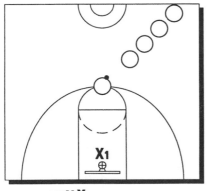

Diagram 9-2

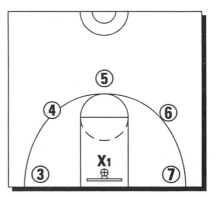

Diagram 9-3

Coaches should emphasize several points during this drill:

- Good shooting is a matter of concentrating and not being distracted by the defender.
- Good defense on shooters mean distracting the shooters and breaking their concentration without fouling.
- Making open shots, particularly lay-ups, is the key to winning offensive basketball.
- Getting a shot off quickly after receiving a pass is another key to good shooting. The coach should emphasize receiving the ball in bent knee position, while stepping toward the pass, using a one to two step approach to the incoming pass.
- The coach should not allow the defender to make poor passes to the offensive player. Passers should make a crisp, two-handed chest pass to the shooter. If the pass does not arrive at the receiver's chest, the pass should be made again.

What is a Bad Shot?
Coaches should teach their players more than basketball techniques and skills; they should also teach them basketball principles and philosophy. When teaching shooting, coaches should explain to players the difference between a good shot and a bad shot. Good shots and bad shots may vary from player to player, but the determination is always made according to the same rules.

A bad shot is...
- A shot at which the player is not proficient
- A shot taken when the player is off-balance
- A shot taken when the defense has a hand in the player's face
- A shot which the player is forced to change in mid-air
- A shot which does not come within the framework of the offense
- A shot taken but never practiced in practice situations
- A shot taken when fatigued
- A shot taken when the player is not in shot rhythm (for example, when the player fumbled the ball or stumbled)
- A shot taken when a teammate has a better shot and is open
- A shot taken without considering the game situation or time element
- A shot taken when a player has just come off the bench and is not in the flow of the game
- A shot taken when there are no teammates ready to rebound

Mental Aspects of Shooting

Besides the physical techniques, there are many mental aspects to good shooting. To make their players into good shooters, coaches should also address these factors.

Coaches should motivate players to practice on their own. One way to improve players' motivation is to help them create a good self-image. Coaches should not simply berate a player for missing or taking a poor shot. Instead, they should explain to the player why the shot was missed (the errors in technique or form) or why the shot was a poor shot.

Coaches should also help players set realistic shooting goals. These goals will vary depending on the age and ability of the player. For example, a player's goal might be to shoot 50 lay-ups three times a week, to never be short with a shot, or to make three straight shots from a specific spot in practice before moving to a different area.

It is also important for coaches to help their players visualize when shooting. They can tell players about the size of the rim, that it is big enough for three balls to fit into it at the same time (Photo 9-22). Showing players how big the rim is can increase their confidence in their ability to make a basket. Coaches might also tell players to visualize the ball going over the rim and the net swishing as the shot goes through it (Photo 9-23), or to imagine a target on the rim (Photo 9-24).

Photo 9-22

Photo 9-23

By helping players to relax and use various visualization exercises, coaches can make youngsters better shooters.

To become an effective player and a great shooter, players should be able to make a greater percentage of shots than ever before. When there is no one guarding them, they should be able to hit 60 to 70 percent of their shots in practice depending on their age. They should learn to shoot properly even when they are tired and their concentration begins to waver. They should also have a shooting spot, a favorite area on the floor from which they know they can always make a shot, and a "bread and butter" shot, a favorite shot they know they can always make. Finally, they should learn to concentrate. They should be able to hit six to eight shots in a row. Ideally, when players are practicing without anyone guarding them, they should never miss more than three shots in a row.

Photo 9-24

Eight-Minute Drill

Players should shoot 50 to 100 shots from a particular spot without stopping. They should be able to shoot the 100 shots in about eight minutes. To really work hard, players should shoot, retrieve their own rebound, and dribble back out to their spot.

Players could have a partner to chart their shots. The chart should have the numbers 1 through 100 written on it in order. If the shot is missed, the partner puts a slash through the number. If the shot is made, the partner circles the number. Players can then total their field goal percentage, most consecutive made shots, and most consecutive missed shots.

This drill should be performed at least three times a week. It is easy for players to cheat or slack off, but they are only hurting themselves. If players are committed to becoming great shooters, they will take the drill seriously. A sample shooting chart is on the following page.

What Makes a Good Shooter?

1. Correct form and technique
2. Countless hours of practice
3. Having the right mental approach
4. Accountability

Date _____

FGA ___ FGM ___

Consecutive makes _____

Consecutive misses _____

1	2	3	4	5	6	7	8	9	10	11	12	13	14	15
16	17	18	19	20	21	22	23	24	25	26	27	28	29	30
31	32	33	34	35	36	37	38	39	40	41	42	43	44	45
46	47	48	49	50	51	52	53	54	55	56	57	58	59	60
61	62	63	64	65	66	67	68	69	70	71	72	73	74	75
76	77	78	79	80	81	82	83	84	85	86	87	88	89	90
91	92	93	94	95	96	97	98	99	100					

Date _____

FGA ___ FGM ___

Consecutive makes _____

Consecutive misses _____

1	2	3	4	5	6	7	8	9	10	11	12	13	14	15
16	17	18	19	20	21	22	23	24	25	26	27	28	29	30
31	32	33	34	35	36	37	38	39	40	41	42	43	44	45
46	47	48	49	50	51	52	53	54	55	56	57	58	59	60
61	62	63	64	65	66	67	68	69	70	71	72	73	74	75
76	77	78	79	80	81	82	83	84	85	86	87	88	89	90
91	92	93	94	95	96	97	98	99	100					

Date _____

FGA ___ FGM ___

Consecutive makes _____

Consecutive misses _____

1	2	3	4	5	6	7	8	9	10	11	12	13	14	15
16	17	18	19	20	21	22	23	24	25	26	27	28	29	30
31	32	33	34	35	36	37	38	39	40	41	42	43	44	45
46	47	48	49	50	51	52	53	54	55	56	57	58	59	60
61	62	63	64	65	66	67	68	69	70	71	72	73	74	75
76	77	78	79	80	81	82	83	84	85	86	87	88	89	90
91	92	93	94	95	96	97	98	99	100					

For Free Throw Concentration:

The Perfect Free Throw: One which swishes or hits back part of rim and comes right back to the shooter

Recording Free Throws: The perfect free throw ●
Made but not perfect ╱
Missed free throw ○

Individual Shooting Practice
Coaches use drills in practice to teach shooting. Players should also practice on their own. There are several drills players can use when practicing alone to improve their shot.

Spot Shooting Versus the Pro
Players should pick a spot and take 25 shots from that spot. They should then take 25 shots from the spot off one hard dribble; 25 shots off two hard dribbles; and 25 shots after a good head, ball, and foot fake. They should keep track of the number of shots made and award themselves one point for every shot they make. Michael Jordan is awarded two points for every shot they miss.

	Sample Chart		
Date	**Shots Taken**	**My Score**	**Michael Jordan's Score**
June 2	100	60	80
June 3	50	35	30
June 4	100	55	90
June 5	100	71	58

On June 2, for example, the player made 60 shots for 60 points. The player missed 40 shots, so Jordan was given 80 points. To win, players must make 67 percent of their shots.

Zero Backwards
Players pick one or more spots to shoot from and choose a number (six, for example) to start with. They subtract one for every shot they make and add one for every shot they miss. They should practice until they reach zero.

Form Concentration
Using the basketball shooting checklist, players should choose one of the techniques to emphasize. For example, a player may focus on keeping the elbow tucked in, positioning of the wrist on the follow-through, or releasing the ball properly. The players then check that point on every shot they take.

Time Yourself
Players should shoot consecutive shots for five or ten minutes, keeping track of how many they make or miss. Their goal should be to make 65 percent of their shots. Players should keep their practice goals high because shooting percentages

always drop during game competition. If players can not make 50 percent of their shots in practice, they will certainly not shoot well when someone is guarding them. Again, age will determine these percentage goals.

Videotape Yourself
Players should ask someone to videotape their shooting and then go over the video with the help of their shooting checklist. Players should watch the video in slow motion and critique themselves on each point: triple-threat position, the set up, the head and eyes, the grip, and the shot and finish. By studying themselves on tape, players will learn to analyze their shot and correct problems.

Becoming Familiar With the Basketball
Players should place a strip of tape around the center of the ball. At times when they are not practicing, they can condition their hands and fingers to grip the ball correctly by tossing the ball 6 to 12 inches in the air and catching it with their index and middle fingers straddling the tape.

Free Throws
Players should begin by shooting 10 consecutive free throws. If they do not make seven or more, they must shoot 10 more. As they improve, players can switch to shooting 20 consecutive free throws, of which they must make 15.

Players should always end their individual practice with 10 hard sprints the length of the court, or with two minutes of rope jumping or jumping to touch the rim or net.

Free Throw Shooting
The mental game is extremely important in free throw shooting. Coaches should emphasize to their players that the shot is called a free throw for a reason; there is no defender guarding the shooter and trying to distract him. The shot is always taken from the same spot on the court: in the middle of the floor 15 feet from the basket. In free throw shooting, players can concentrate on muscle memory reflex, developing the same routine and the same muscle reaction for the shot every time. There is nothing to force the shooters to change their practice routine.

It is important for shooters to develop a free throw routine to help them catch their breath, relax, and focus. This routine should involve what players do before stepping to the line as well as what they do after accepting the ball from the referee. For example, players might close their eyes for a couple seconds and visualize the rim and the ball passing through it before stepping to the line. After accepting the ball, players might bounce it three times, spin it in their hand, and come to a complete stop before beginning their shot. All shooting techniques also apply to shooting free throws (Photos 9-25 through 9-28).

Photo 9-25

Photo 9-26

Photo 9-27

Photo 9-28

Common Mistakes in Shooting the Basketball

Teaching young players the art of shooting the basketball can be an overwhelming task. Before beginning, coaches should be aware of the mistakes commonly made by youngsters.

- Smaller or weaker players often do not get their arms into the shot. They bend their legs, but put the ball up too quickly with the arms. The arms and legs are both sources of power, and should work together.
- Young players often put the wrong foot forward. Right-handed shooters should have the right foot slightly in front of the left. Left-handed shooters should have the left foot slightly in front of the right.
- The player's shoulders are not square to the basket.
- The player's eyes follow the shot while it is in the air, snapping the head backward. This motion causes a jerk in the release.
- The player's wrist is not cocked, and the ball is pushed outward or slung toward the basket rather than being pushed upward. The same problem occurs if the elbow is not pointed at the basket.
- The player's arm is not straight at the conclusion of the shot, nor is the wrist bent on the follow-through.
- The player shoots without bending the legs. If the legs are not bent, they do not supply any power to the shot.
- Players do not release the shot quickly enough. They spend too much time aiming, often "measuring" the shot. As a result of this slow release, their shot is blocked.

When players shoot the basketball, there should be little or no movement of the head. Snapping the head back, swinging the shoulders to the side, and shuffling the feet should all be avoided. These actions do nothing but destroy the smoothness and consistency of the shot.

Once players understand the proper techniques, the key element is repetition. To be consistently good shooters, players must repeatedly practice shooting properly. This repetition is especially important for free throws.

Concentration and mental discipline are critical to good shooting. Players can not allow the defense to distract them, and they must also learn to fight fatigue, game pressure, the crowd, and themselves. Mental discipline is especially important in free throw shooting. Players should not be allowed to talk while shooting free throws in practice. It is also important for coaches to help their players develop confidence and a positive mental attitude when it comes to shooting. A combination of enthusiasm, hard work, and goal setting equals success.

CHAPTER 10

Tips For Coaches

Coaching youth basketball requires much more than knowledge of the X's and O's of the game. Setting up an effective practice plan requires a great deal of preparation. Working with young players involves more than simply teaching them the necessary techniques; coaches must first help them develop the necessary agility and coordination. Youth coaches should also be prepared to deal with the fragile egos and self images of children.

Coaching youth basketball means more than winning and losing, developing skills, and creating a fun environment. It also means building relationships that exist beyond the basketball season. Youth basketball coaches create impressions that can last the rest of a player's life.

Young athletes look up to their coaches. They expect their coaches to be examples of sportsmanship, hard work, dedication, responsibility, and fairness. This responsibility is the single most important task of the youth basketball coach, but too many coaches do not take it seriously.

Questions Coaches Must Answer
There are several questions, whether spoken or unspoken, that youth coaches owe their players answers to:

- Do you know what you are talking about?
- Can I trust you?
- Do you value me as a person, not just an athlete who plays basketball?
- Are you committed to the team?

If coaches can answer "yes" to all these questions, they can not fail. Coaches are teachers, and they have a unique opportunity to influence the attitudes and character of young people. Basketball players and coaches experience a wide range of emotions: determination, anticipation, exhilaration, joy, disappointment, frustration, and bitterness. Each day presents an opportunity for players to recognize, handle, and learn from these experiences. Therefore, the coach has the responsibility of being prepared for such opportunities.

Coaches should always be concerned about the safety and welfare of each individual player. The health and well-being of the athlete should always take precedence over anything else, and coaches should always consider these factors before making decisions. This concern for a player's welfare does not end with physical well-being; the psychological health of an athlete is also crucial.

Coaches are responsible for emphasizing sportsmanship, motivation, self-discipline, loyalty, leadership, and team play to their athletes. Team sports present an opportunity for youngsters to learn to work together to accomplish goals. Coaches should encourage players to be the best they can be, but the goal of youth sports should never be to win at all costs.

Coaches should explain to all team members and their parents the importance of safety, proper care of equipment and uniforms, and team rules. It is a good idea to hold a pre-season meeting which all players must attend with at least one of their parents. Coaches should inform everyone of all team guidelines, particularly those regarding promptness; acceptable language and conduct; the treatment of teammates, opponents, and referees; and, with older players, the use of alcohol and drugs. Rules should be enforced fairly and consistently. When dealing with younger players, coaches should speak in terms they can understand. Good communication between coaches and players, and coaches and parents at this pre-season meeting will minimize problems during the season. Youth coaches should remember parents are entrusting them with their greatest treasure: their sons and daughters.

The following are some recommendations to help coaches become the most effective coach they can be and fulfill their responsibilities to their players.

- Coaches should dress appropriately for coaching basketball. Sweatpants or shorts, an appropriate shirt, and tennis shoes or basketball shoes are essential. Coaches who do not look like coaches immediately lose the respect of their players.
- Coaches should be the first to arrive for and the last to leave a practice or game. They should also come prepared.
- Coaches should not smoke in the presence of their squad.
- Coaches should not curse or use demeaning language.
- Coaches should be as positive as possible. When they criticize, they should follow it up with a compliment. They should not embarrass their players.
- Coaches should demand respect from their players, both for themselves and for any other authority figure speaking to them.
- Coaches should build spirit by example. They should applaud good effort and hustle and single out players who make a good pass or get a tough rebound.

They should praise players for improving a specific skill, and not simply look at points scored or the good players on the team.

- Coaches should not abuse or criticize the officials. When players see their coaches behave in this manner, they also begin to behave that way.
- Coaches should not make excuses for losses or poor play.
- Coaches should talk to fellow coaches. They should always be willing to listen and learn when they talk to opposing coaches or coaches whom they respect. No one knows it all. Sharing ideas with others helps people learn and grow.

There have been many studies regarding youth sports. According to surveys, the following are the seven most important reasons youngsters plays sports:

1. To have fun
2. To improve skills
3. For the excitement of competition
4. To do something they are good at
5. To stay in shape
6. For the challenge of competition
7. To be part of a team or to be with their friends

Parents and coaches alike should notice that winning is not one of the reasons given.

When players leave a team at the end of a season, the coach's goal should be for them to have had a great experience. Coaches should want them to always remember their time on the team as fun, challenging, and meaningful. The greatest compliment of all is when a player's parents tell the coach their child really learned important lessons about basketball and life.

Rich Grawer was the head men's basketball coach of the St. Louis University Billikens for 10 years. During that time he averaged 16 wins per season, and twice finished second in the NIT tournament. Grawer holds the Billikens record for most wins in a single season with 27, and is widely credited with developing the basketball program into what it is today. Prior to becoming head coach at St. Louis University, Grawer was an assistant coach at the University of Missouri-Columbia. During his college coaching career he coached several future NBA players, including Anthony Bonner and Steve Stipanovich. Before joining the college ranks, Grawer spent 12 years as the coach at DeSmet High School in St. Louis, posting a record of 270-87 that included three state championships and a 63-game winning streak.

Now the athletic director at Clayton High School, Grawer is in demand as a speaker and holds clinics across the nation and around the world. He and his wife, Theresa, live in St. Louis with their six children, all of whom played youth and high school basketball. Three of their children—Kevin, Brian, and Rick—received college basketball scholarships.

Sally Tippett Rains has co-authored several sports books including *Youth Baseball: A Coach's and Parent's Guide* with Wendell Kim and *Softball Pitching Fundamentals and Techniques* with Carie Dever-Boaz. She and her husband, Rob Rains, wrote *Playing on His Team*, a book about role model athletes. Her background includes working as a sports writer for KMOX Radio in St. Louis and writing several articles for *The Sporting News*.

Rains is a writing coach at Webster University in St. Louis, where she lives with husband, Rob, and her two sons, B.J. and Mike.